Amazing Animals
Wolves

Please visit our Web site, www.garethstevens.com. For a free color catalog of all our high-quality books, call toll free 1-800-542-2595 or fax 1-877-542-2596.

Library of Congress Cataloging-in-Publication Data

Wilsdon, Christina.
  Wolves / Christina Wilsdon.
    p. cm. — (Amazing animals)
  Includes index.
  ISBN 978-1-4339-4032-3 (pbk.)
  ISBN 978-1-4339-4033-0 (6-pack)
  ISBN 978-1-4339-4031-6 (library binding) —
  1. Wolves—Juvenile literature. I. Title.
  QL737.C22W545 2010
  599.773—dc22
                        2010000493

This edition first published in 2011 by
Gareth Stevens Publishing
111 East 14th Street, Suite 349
New York, NY 10003

This edition copyright © 2011 Gareth Stevens Publishing.
Original edition copyright © 2006 by Readers' Digest Young Families.

Editor: Greg Roza
Designer: Christopher Logan

Photo credits: Cover, p. 25 (bottom right), backcover Shutterstock.com; pp. 1, 3, 4–5, 18–19, 28 (top left), 42–43, 46 © Corel Corporation; pp. 6–7 Stephen J. Krasemann; pp. 8–9, 30–31 © Image 100 Ltd.; p. 9 Daniel J. Cox/Getty Images; pp. 10 (bottom), 10–11, 12–13, 13 (bottom right), 14–15, 22–23, 24–25, 26–27, 36–37, 40, 44–45 © Dynamic Graphics Inc.; pp. 16–17 © Corbis; pp. 20–21, 38–39 © PhotoDisc; pp. 28–29, 32–33, 34–35 © Digital Vision.

Printed in the United States of America

CPSIA compliance information: Batch #CS10GS: For further information contact Gareth Stevens, New York, New York at 1-800-542-2595.

Amazing Animals
Wolves

By Christina Wilsdon

Gareth Stevens
Publishing

Contents

Chapter 1
Wolf Pups Grow Up

A **pack** of gray wolves huddles together on a cold morning in early spring. One wolf is snug and warm in a den underground. Her furry body curls around five newborn pups. Each fuzzy brown pup is just 6 inches (15 cm) long.

The pups can't see, because their eyes are still tightly shut. They can't hear or walk yet, either. They can only creep by pulling themselves along with their front legs. Scrabbling and shoving, the pups snuggle against their mother. Then they settle down as they drink her warm milk.

The mother wolf will live in the den with her pups for almost a month. She will go outside only to pass waste and drink water. Her mate and the other wolves in the pack will bring her food.

Growing Pups

A wolf pup weighs about 1 pound (0.5 kg) when born. It gains 2 to 3 pounds (1 to 1.5 kg) a week during the first 14 weeks of its life.

After 2 weeks, the pups open their blue eyes. They can walk now, and their baby teeth are growing. When they are 3 weeks old, they leave the den for the first time. The rest of the pack sniffs the pups from nose to tail.

All the wolves in the pack help care for the pups. They guard them as they play outside the den. One of the adults will even babysit the pups if the mother goes hunting with the pack. The wolves help feed the pups, too. They carry food in their stomachs to the pups. When the pups lick a wolf's mouth, it coughs up the food for them.

By 9 weeks, the pups eat only meat. They look more like adult wolves now, but their heads and feet are still too big for their bodies. Their coats are a mixture of puppy fuzz and adult fur.

Baby Blues

A wolf pup's blue eyes turn yellow by the time it is 4 months old.

Play Time

For the first few weeks of life, the pups' world is limited to the area outside their den. They chase mice and chew sticks. They wrestle and romp. They climb on adult wolves that are trying to nap!

When the pups are a little older, their world grows a bit bigger. They travel with the pack to a new area called a **rendezvous site**. Now the pups can explore an even bigger area. For the next few weeks, this site will be the pack's meeting place. Then they will all move to a different rendezvous site.

By the time the pups are 6 months old, they are nearly as big as adult wolves. They are strong enough to learn the hunting skills they need to survive.

Their first winter is harsh and cold, but deer are plentiful. The pups eat well and grow stronger. In spring, the year-old pups are fully grown at last. Now they help bring food to their mother as she raises a new **litter** in the old den.

Home Wolf or Lone Wolf?

A wolf has a decision to make when it grows up. It can stay with the pack and help raise the young. Or it can leave when it is about 2 years old and find a mate. It strikes out to find a new home.

Chapter 2
The Body of a Wolf

A wolf's paw can be as much as 5.5 inches (14 cm) long. Tough pads and long claws help the wolf climb rocks and grip the ground when it runs.

Wild Dogs

The wolf is the **ancestor** of all dogs. Some dogs, such as huskies, look a lot like wolves. Other dogs, such as poodles, don't.

Gray wolves are the biggest wild dogs. A large male wolf can be 6 feet (1.8 m) long from nose to tail. He can be about 3 feet (0.9 m) tall! Much of this height comes from a wolf's legs. Long legs are good for running. Scientists have recorded wolves **sprinting** at speeds up to 30 miles (48 km) per hour.

A wolf can run at top speed for only a little while. But it can trot for many hours at 5 miles (8 km) per hour. It can also lope at 20 miles (32 km) per hour for about 20 minutes while chasing **prey**. Why does a wolf need to be a good runner? Because it eats deer, moose, and **caribou**— animals that run even faster!

Long Jump

A wolf can leap 16 feet (4.9 m) in a single bound— about half the length of a school bus!

Wolf Senses

A wolf uses its sharp senses to find food. Its sense of smell is especially keen. Wolves can smell other animals from a distance of about 300 yards (274 m). One scientist watched a pack of wolves catch the scent of moose that were 1.5 miles (2.4 km) away!

A wolf also has excellent hearing. It can hear a wolf that is howling several miles (km) away. Each ear can swivel in different directions to locate the source of a sound.

Wolves are good at spotting movement and seeing in low light. This helps wolves hunt when it's dark, but they are not able to pick out details. A wolf's eyes are positioned toward the front of its head. This helps the wolf judge distances. A deer's eyes are on the sides of its head. This helps it see in multiple directions without moving its head. This allows the deer to watch for danger—such as a hungry wolf!

My, What Big Teeth You Have...

Wolves are **carnivores**—meat eaters. Like all carnivores, adult wolves have strong, sharp teeth. An adult wolf has 42 teeth, including four sharp fangs for holding on to prey.

Wolves are lucky to have sensitive ears and noses to help them find food, because their eyesight is not very sharp.

Pups from the same litter sometimes grow adult coats that are different colors.

Coat of Many Colors

Gray wolves are not always gray. They can be white, creamy, or black. Their coats can also be shades of brown, tan, and red. Even a gray wolf's "gray" fur is made up of different shades of gray sprinkled with white, brown, and black. Wolves that live in the far north tend to be lighter in color than wolves farther south. Wolves in the forests farther south are usually gray or black.

A wolf gets its color from the long, stiff hairs on its coat called guard hairs. These hairs grow 4 to 5 inches (10 to 13 cm) long on its shoulders and back. They work like a raincoat to shed water. Closer to the wolf's skin is a layer of short, fluffy fur that keeps it warm.

> ## Winter Coat
>
> A wolf's fur is thick enough to protect it from temperatures below freezing. A wolf in a snowstorm stays warm by curling up and tucking its nose between its hind legs, then covering its face with its tail.

Gray wolf pups are born with fuzzy brown or gray coats. They change into their adult colors when they begin to grow adult hairs.

Chapter 3
Wolf Packs

Wolf packs have fewer than 20 wolves. Usually, packs are only four to eight wolves.

Life in the Wild

A wolf can live alone. However, a wolf's life is easier and safer if it is part of a pack. The pack is the wolf's family. It is usually made up of two parents and their young. Some packs also include aunts, uncles, or unrelated wolves.

All the wolves in a pack work together to catch food and take care of the pups. They defend their home, or **territory**, from other wolves. A pack's territory is where it **roams**, hunts, and raises its young.

Top Dogs

The leader of the pack is a strong male wolf called the **alpha male**. His mate is known as the alpha female. The alpha wolves are the only pair in the pack that mate and have pups.

The other wolves in the pack obey the alphas. However, each wolf has its own place above or below the other wolves. This place is called a rank. A wolf can only boss around, or dominate, a wolf of lower rank. A ranking system like this is called a **dominance order**.

Family Life

A dominance order helps wolves get along with one another. Each wolf knows its place so the pack can work together and survive. Still, wolves in a pack sometimes quarrel. If you watch a pack of wolves, you may see bared teeth and hear snarls and growls. Wolves use body language to be friendly, too. An adult wolf may greet its father by acting like a puppy begging for food. You may also see wagging tails and friendly licks. These behaviors are all part of how wolves communicate.

Wolves also "talk" with their tails. A dominant wolf holds its tail high in the air. A low-ranking wolf holds its tail down. Wolves also wag their tails when they are being friendly, just as dogs do.

Let's Play!

Has a dog ever bowed to you with its tail up in the air? This action is called a play bow and it means "Let's play!" Wolves play bow when they want to have fun, too.

An angry wolf may bare its teeth and hold its ears straight up, like the wolf on the left. A frightened wolf may lay its ears back flat, like the wolf on the right.

Baby's First Howl

A wolf pup can howl when it is just 2 weeks old.

A wolf that is by itself may use a special "lonesome howl" to call its pack.

Owoooo!

Wolves use sounds to communicate. They are most famous for howling. A wolf's howl is a long, slow song. Other wolves often join in. Scientists have found that humans can hear a wolf's howl from about 4 miles (6.4 km) away. Most likely, a wolf can hear a howl from an even greater distance.

Howling brings the pack together. It helps pack members keep in touch when they are separated. Howling may also remind other packs to stay out of the wolves' territory.

Sniff!

Have you ever walked a dog and had to wait while it stopped to sniff almost every tree? Pet dogs mark territory with urine to communicate with other dogs. Wolves do, too. This behavior is called scent marking. A wolf may also rub its body on objects and scratch the ground to leave its scent.

Wolves mark trees, rocks, and other objects in their territory. These scent marks mean "No trespassing!" Scent marking may be a way of "building fences" between the territories of different packs.

Chapter 4
Hungry as a Wolf

A pack of wolves on the chase look **ferocious**, but the wolves will give up running after a few miles (km). They may also give up if an animal fights back.

Teamwork

Wolves in a pack work as a team to hunt large animals such as moose, deer, elk, sheep, bison, caribou, and musk oxen. Sometimes the wolves see smaller prey before the prey sees the wolves. Then they sneak up on the animals. Other times wolves may see a herd from a hilltop or surprise a sleeping animal.

When wolves get close to their prey, they creep toward it. The prey may not notice the danger until the wolves suddenly rush at it. Once in a while, however, the prey refuses to run away! A strong moose may stand and stare at the wolves until they give up.

Most often, wolves attack animals that are young, old, sick, or injured. These are the easiest animals to catch because they are the weakest and cannot keep up with the herd. However, wolves are strong and fast enough to catch healthy animals, too.

Wolves in the Web

Wolves help keep the food web in their **habitat** balanced. If they weren't around, the animals they hunt would become too numerous. This would put a strain on other parts of the habitat.

Time to Eat

Wolves start eating as soon as a kill is made. They tear at the meat with their fangs and "wolf" it down. A hungry wolf can pack 20 pounds (9 kg) of meat into its stretchy stomach. The alpha wolves do not make other wolves wait until they are done, as male lions do. If the catch is small, however, then the alpha wolves may eat first.

Sometimes wolves try to snatch food from one another. But rank doesn't matter when a wolf has food in its jaws. A young wolf doesn't have to give food to an older wolf. If food is hard to find, however, the parents may boss around the older wolves to make sure the pups are well fed.

On the Prowl

Wolves can hunt any time of day, but their favorite times are at dawn or dusk. Many wolf hunts also take place at night.

After a meal, the pack rests. The wolves need to get their energy back after a chase. Resting also gives their bodies time to digest food. A wolf digests its food quickly, so it may eat again in just a few hours. A wolf eats all it can when food is available. That way, it can survive when there is no food. If hunting is poor, a wolf pack may go for 2 weeks without eating.

The whole wolf pack eats
at the same time when the
prey is large.

Hungry wolves don't hunt only big prey, such as deer. Wolves often eat beavers and hares. They can even survive on mice!

A Web of Life

Deer, moose, and other prey are not the only animals in the wolf's world. Wolves also share their habitat with animals that are not prey—including other **predators**. In some places, these predators are bears. Most of the time, bears and wolves have nothing to do with one another. But if a bear stumbles across a wolf pack's prey, the wolves usually run away. The bear gets a free meal!

Mountain lions and coyotes have a more difficult time with wolves. Scientists recently found that wolves in Montana chase mountain lions away from their meals. Wolves do not get along with coyotes at all and will chase and even kill them.

Bird Games

Ravens seem to have a special bond with wolves. They follow wolves when they see them hunting. The big black birds even fly above wolf trails, looking for wolves. Wolves sometimes seem to play with ravens. The birds tease the wolves into leaping at them and fly away at the last second. Then the ravens start the game again!

Chapter 5
Wolves in the World

Scientists and others help persuade people that these wild dogs are not the "big bad wolves" of fairy tales.

Where Wolves Live

The green area shows where wolves live today.

Just 200 years ago, many kinds of gray wolves roamed North America. Some lived as far south as Mexico. A different **species**, the red wolf, lived in the southeastern United States.

Europeans who came to North America in the 1600s feared wolves and offered rewards for killing them.

The killing increased in the 1800s. By the 1960s, just a few hundred wolves remained in Minnesota and Michigan.

Today, large numbers of gray wolves still live in Alaska and Canada. Some live in parts of the northern United States. Gray wolves also live in parts of Europe and Asia.

The Future of Wolves

Wolves have lost much of their habitat as the human population has grown. Laws now protect their homes. Fortunately, wolves are very **adaptable**. As long as they have enough room to roam and hunt prey, they can live in prairies, forests, woods, and **tundra**.

Most North American wolves still live in Canada, Alaska, and parts of northern Minnesota, Michigan, and Wisconsin. But now their howls can sometimes be heard in parts of Washington, Idaho, Montana, Wyoming, North Dakota, and South Dakota.

Fast Facts About Gray Wolves

Scientific name	*Canis lupus*
Class	Mammals
Order	Carnivora
Size	Up to 3 feet (0.9 m) tall at the shoulder
Weight	Males to 110 pounds (50 kg) Females to 90 pounds (41 kg)
Life span	About 10 years in the wild About 13 years in captivity
Habitat	Forests, woods, tundra, and prairies
Top Speed	About 30 miles (48 km) per hour

The Dog Family

Wolves are part of a scientific family called *Canidae*. This family is made up of 34 species, which include domestic dogs, wild dogs, wolves, coyotes, and foxes.

Glossary

adaptable—able to adjust easily to new conditions

alpha male—a wolf that is leader in its pack

ancestor—an animal from whom others are descended

caribou—reindeer

carnivore—an animal that eats meat

dominance order—a system in which some wolves in a pack have a higher rank than others

ferocious—fierce, savage

habitat—the natural environment where an animal or plant lives

litter—a group of pups born at the same time

pack—a family or group of wolves that live together

predator—an animal that hunts and eats other animals to survive

prey—animals that are hunted by other animals for food

rendezvous site—an area used by a pack of wolves with young pups

roam—to wander

species—a category of living things that are the same kind

sprint—to run as fast as possible for a short distance

territory—an area defended by a wolf pack

tundra—cold, snowy northern lands that lack forests

Wolves: Show What You Know

How much have you learned about wolves? Grab a piece of paper and a pencil and write your answers down.

1. How many teeth does an adult wolf have?

2. What color are a wolf cub's eyes?

3. How fast can a wolf sprint?

4. What are a wolf's two sharpest senses?

5. How many wolves are usually found in a typical pack?

6. Which wolf is the alpha male?

7. Why do wolves mark their territory with their scents?

8. How much food can a hungry adult wolf eat in one meal?

9. Where do most North American wolves live?

10. How long do gray wolves live in the wild?

1. 42 2. Blue 3. About 30 miles (48 km) per hour 4. Smell and hearing 5. Four to eight wolves 6. The strong male wolf that leads a pack 7. To warn other wolf packs not to trespass in their territory 8. About 20 pounds (9 kg) 9. Alaska and Canada 10. About 10 years

For More Information

Books

Brandenburg, Jim, and Judy Brandenburg. *Face to Face with Wolves*. Washington, DC: National Geographic, 2008.

Markle, Sandra. *Wolves*. Minneapolis, MN: Carolrhoda Books, 2004.

Wimmer, Teresa. *Wolves*. Mankato, MN: Creative Education, 2010.

Web Sites

National Geographic: Wolf

animals.nationalgeographic.com/animals/mammals/wolf.html

Learn about wolves and their habitats from National Geographic.

International Wolf Center

www.wolf.org

The Web site for the International Wolf Center in Ely, Minnesota, has a lot of information about wolves, their habitats, and how to protect them from harm.

Index

A
alpha female 25, 34
alpha male 25, 34

B
body language 26

C
Canidae 43
Canis lupus 42
carnivores 18
coats 10, 20, 21
communicate 26, 29

D
den 9, 10, 12, 13
dogs 17, 26, 29, 40, 43
dominance order 25, 26

E
ears 18, 19, 27
eyes 9, 10, 18

F
food web 33

G
gray wolves 17, 21, 41, 42
guard hairs 21

H
habitat 33, 37, 42
hearing 18, 29
howl 18, 28, 29, 42
hunting 10, 13, 18, 25, 33, 34, 37, 42

L
legs 9, 17, 21
litter 13, 20

M
mate 9, 13, 25

P
pack 9, 10, 13, 18, 24, 25, 26, 28, 29, 32, 33, 34, 35, 37
paw 16
play bow 26
predators 37
prey 17, 18, 33, 35, 36, 37, 42
pups 9, 10, 12, 13, 20, 21, 25, 28, 34

R
rank 25, 26, 34
ravens 37
red wolf 41
rendezvous site 13

S
scent marking 29
smell 18
species 41, 43

T
tail 10, 17, 21, 26
teeth 10, 18, 26, 27
territory 25, 29